Andrew's Poetic Expressions Of God And Love

Andrew Guidry

Presentation by *BookLeaf Publishing*

Web: www.bookleafpub.com

E-mail: info@bookleafpub.com

ISBN: 9789358366310

First edition 2023

*I dedicate this book to God and my Lord
and Savior Jesus Christ.*

ACKNOWLEDGEMENT

I am grateful to my wife, who has always been by my side, and to BookLeaf Publishing for giving me this awesome opportunity to share my gift of poetry to the world.

PREFACE

As a youth, I was told by an English teacher that I was a great suspense writer. That thought would have me believe I could write rap lyrics and become rich. After writing what I was told was good rap lyrics, a great uneasiness fell upon me and I felt I didn't want to be known this way. I would later meet an ordained minister who introduced me to the Holy Bible in a way that would change my life. My writings would then become poems of love for God and humanity.

Heavenly Thoughts

Early this morning,
when I opened my eyes,
heavenly thoughts filled my mind
as I watched the sunrise
and when I stepped outside onto my porch
to feel how the day would begin
I was greeted by a strong, northern wind.
It said to me
continue to live righteously
and strive to be sin free
in my mind
I knew this was God talking to me,
telling me in my heart
is where I would find a key,
that would unlock a door
to inner peace,
that dwells within not just me,
but within all humanity,
this is where the world can find unity,
the sun rays said to me
as they soaked into my golden brown skin filling
me
with enormous amounts of energy.
Learn to love yourself,
and then you can learn to love someone else

was the wisdom bestowed upon me
from those warm streaks of heat
I then lifted my head
to take in a fresh breath.
I can smell the rain coming,
my soul wants to get wet
with wisdom and knowledge,
answers to questions found in my heart,
but studied in college,
and as my heavenly thoughts
continue to roll on with infinite mileage,
I was told
by those cold
drops of rain
that wisdom is a gift from God,
something every man can,
but won't attain
so study the word of God
and for you, they will explain
Now this brought
my thoughts
back to when I was lame,
ashamed
because a man would talk to me
about the word of God,
but all I knew about
was the drug game,
but as time progressed,
I was blessed

with an understanding
that became vigorously demanding
for the truth
I became in tune with the moon
that mentioned to me
not to live my life selfishly,
but to use this understanding
in the midst of my poetry
to try and reach out to you
so just as sure as the stars
shines bright into the night,
a righteous heart
and heavenly thoughts
will guide you to an eternal life.

True Love

Love is a top priority in life
and one of its best results
is when a man and a woman
becomes husband and wife.
Their connection is as sharp as a knife
cutting through all the red tape
that would keep them from soaring
the heights of a kite
Love is an inspiration,
it inspires me to write
about how it makes you feel
when the love you're receiving is real
you would know
because old wounds begin to heal,
It's not tangible
but yet it's something you can feel
Love, can you understand this word,
A feeling from within
that demands to be heard
or felt by whom it is well deserved.
Sometimes you can even feel it
in your nerves.
It gives you chills
or goosebumps
small lumps on your skin

from a feeling that comes from deep within.
No, I don't think love is a game,
the feeling is real
even within its name
I wish it fell from the sky like rain,
so we would all feel the same,
starting with the older
to the younger generations
as it spreads across the nations
becoming a compelling obligation
to love one another
no matter what's your skin color
or situation.

Where Are You?

Hey love, where are you?
I've been looking for a while
I've met many who've made me smile,
but they all seem to go out of style,
so where are you,
the true you,
the one who would stick with me like glue
or the sky to the color blue
continuously, showing me
that my love is enough for you,
and never letting go,
because of a natural flow
like a river of love
which consist of
trust, honesty, and respect,
and the love and blessings of God
who would make it a strong connect
between you and I
and we would never say goodbye,
because any problem we encounter,
working them out together
is how we would try
and succeed,
and as long as you and I can breathe,
we would always have a special friendship

within a love we know is true
For this I wait patiently,
but hey love, where are you?

Seek And Ye Shall Find

The year was 1995
when I began to look upon this world
without the use of my naked eyes,
this process revealed to me,
hatred, deceptions, lies,
and a systematic killing
of an entire ethnic group,
in a single term,
genocide.
This malevolent reality
made my soul cringe,
and my flesh began to cry,
I began repetitiously asking myself,
why, why, why?
For a brief moment it appeared to me
the only way out of this world for me
would be to just die,
but I don't believe in committing suicide,
so what should I do?
Find me a hole and hide?
Imminently,
my heart and mind reacted
simultaneously
and the result was me
standing firm

saying no! I'm a strong black man
and I won't be denied
not a minute longer
it became known to me
that the proper terminology
that would best describe
my state of being would be
black pride.
My life became a journey.
I was searching for answers to questions
my heart so deeply desired
at that moment in time
my mind could not find,
but if my journey
led me to the top of Mount Kilimanjaro,
my determination
would only prepare me for that climb.
My journey was complex and challenging,
but when I got to the top of that mountain,
I was no longer blind,
because I found
that you and I
are physical manifestations
of He whom I ventured out to find.

Love Still Exists

We've been seeing each other
for a very short while,
but there is something I'd like to say
I've always loved you,
but I never knew how
to express it without scaring you away
In the beginning,
you said, you weren't looking
for a man to commit
well, my love is real
and my heart is sealed.
Is this too much for you to live with?
Or is my love
too much for you to handle
I promise you my love
is not some heartbreaking scandal.
Don't let it melt away
like a burning candle
love still exists
if you open up and let it in.
Baby, please don't be afraid,
because no games are being played.
I want to show you a part of me
that only you could ever see
I know you've been hurt in the past,

but I can only show you
our love will last
Lady, look me in the eyes
and say you'll give me a chance.
Or is my love
too much for you to handle
I promise you my love
is not some heartbreaking scandal.
Don't let it melt away
like a burning candle
love still exists
if you open up and let it in
Woman, you mean so much to me,
open your heart and trust in me
that I can be all the air you need
now you can exhale
Baby, you can breathe
each and every night
I fall to my knees
praying you to want this opportunity
to spend the rest of your life with me
say yes,
and we will live in harmony,
Or is my love
too much for you to handle
I promise you my love
is not some heartbreaking scandal.
Don't let it melt away
like a burning candle

love still exists
if you open up and let it in.

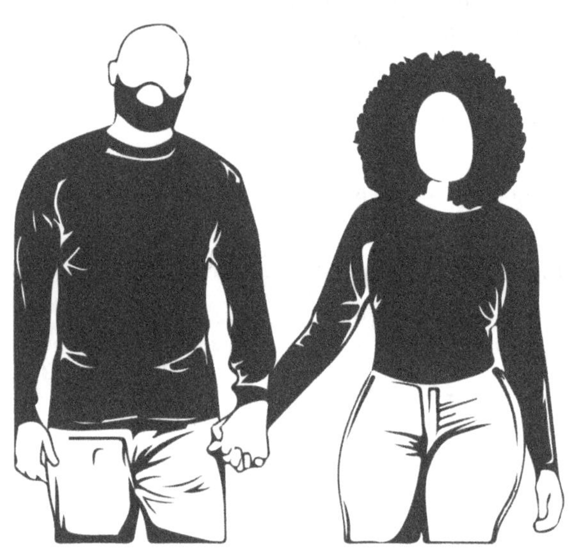

Hey Love

Hey love,
I'm still here
captured by the vigorous grasp of your love,
rushing through my veins,
with the speed of a runaway train,
changing the pace of my heart,
which is sending signals to my brain
that are transforming into my thoughts.
Thoughts of you and how you make me feel is
so good and real
I can't wait until
you come home to me
where you need to be
in my arms holding you tightly,
close to me
staring into your 360 degrees of beauty,
 Baby would you like to know what I see?
I can see the galaxy
in your eyes
followed by the universe
in your smile,
Which is formed by your lips
that are soft
like the clouds in the sky
I see a beautiful woman

possessing what I call
winners pride,
holding her head up high
and ready to find the truth
from within the lies
that we are systematically
forced to live by
a woman with a heart
full of love and affection.
I would definitely say
that you are a blessing
to mother earth
since the beginning of your birth,
when God bestowed upon you
a special key
that allowed you to unlock doors
And give birth to humanity
when I look at you baby,
this is what I see.
I wish you all God's blessings in your future,
with all my love and sincerity.

The Beginning

The Holy Spirit of God
was once hovering over the land,
collecting his thoughts
to begin the world's greatest plan,
which is in the likeness of himself
the creation of a man.
With intelligence unknown to man
he was given form with dust or dirt
from the cleanliness
and the purities
of this earth,
but with this form
man was still incomplete
until the Creator blew into him
the breath of life,
which enabled him to hear, see, speak,
and stand upon his feet
His head was given 360 degrees
of circulation,
such as the earth
from which he was formed
that which contains a key to life
after birth,
which is a oneness
from God, to man, to the earth,

Man was given dominion
over all the creatures of the land,
but he was lonely,
not knowing
that he was only
the beginning of God's Holy plan.

We Can Win

My brothers and sisters
Black, Asian, Hispanic or White,
I"m writing this poem
trying to express unity for our lives.
We've been a divided people
since the beginning of time
when sin fell upon us
and corrupted our minds.
So how do we get our being
to a unified state?
By letting my brothers and sisters
eat off of my plate!
Then putting a fishing pole
in their hands
to show them a way
Each one teach one is my plan.
And then you share with me,
your knowledge and together we
will become our best
Now the divided, corrupt mindsets
are being put to rest.
So basically what I'm saying
is the way that we can win,
is what 1st Peter 4:8 says,
"above all

keep loving one another
earnestly
since love covers
a multitude of sin".

A Message

While living in this world,
I know sometimes things seem hard,
but through all life's trouble,
I find it easy to cope with
when I'm focused on the Lord.
Life seems like it gets
harder by the day
and if I feel I can't t handle it
I don't think about picking up a gun
and blowing my brains away,
I fall to my knees and I pray
Because I know that God
is the creator
of my flesh and of my soul
and if you know, like I know
the life that God gave you and I
is worth far more than
silver, platinum, and gold,
or any other material things
you may find in this world
I feel it's all for a man to make
a financial profit
while he's living in this world.
I know some of you may not agree,
but money don't mean anything to me

I mean, I know it's a necessity,
but I try to never let not having any
get the best of me
because when I look deep within myself,
I feel God is concerned with my heart
and not my wealth
so I strive on a daily basis,
trying to be a righteous man
because we are living in the last days
and the end is close at hand,
so whether that be next year,
tomorrow or even tonight
The question you and I have to ask ourselves is
are we living our lives right?
But when I ponder deeper into life
I can't help but think about my people
how some of us make a little money
and think we are equal
when we're not
look deep within yourselves
and you'll see the plot,
which is to make us feel like our lives
are completely worthless,
If we don't share the same
material things
those so-called high class
elite people got.

God Before Things

My life isn't based on monetary,
but I desire that bag
any car would do
but why not let it be a jag
my eyes are so pierced, I see through the bling,
but my peripheral
sometimes get blinded
from that trillion cut diamond ring.
I can take comfort in a shack
because I have God in my heart,
but I desire a mansion
I had a shack from the start
so I'm gonna continue to walk with God
like I did since my youth,
Matthew 6:33 says,
"Seek ye first the kingdom of God
and his righteousness,
and all these things
shall be added unto you".

What You Make Me Feel Inside

You came into my life
like a thief in the night,
but you don't have to steal my heart because I'm
giving it to you tonight.
You have filled my heart
with all of your love
now making you happy
is all I think of.
How can I begin to describe
what you make me feel inside,
you are so pure and good for me
my love for you multiplies by three
You have shown me something
a lot of men won't see
You have shown me what life
with a woman of faith should be
when I am weak
you are my strength
when I am losing all faith
you help me restore it again
How can I begin to describe
what you make me feel inside
you are so pure and good for me
my love for you multiplies by three

Sweetheart come and take my hand
and listen closely to your man
what I have may not seem like a lot,
but with you,
I would share everything that I got
you're in my heart,
you're on my mind,
you're the mate to my soul
baby take my hand in marriage
and together let's grow old.
How can I begin to describe
what you make me feel inside
you are so pure and good for me
my love for you multiplies by three

What Can I Be

You are the master key
to my lock
can I be the peak
on your mountaintop?
You are the bark on my tree
can I be the fish in your sea?
You are the lifelines in my hand
can I be your balance when you stand?
You are the amusement in my park
can I be the light that covers your dark?
You are the combination to my safe
can I be a smile upon your face?
You are my one to infinity
can I be your A to Z?
Baby, if I'm not any of these things
then tell me, what can I be?

I Pray

I pray my flaws
are bass guitar strings
for you to pluck my perfection.
I pray my mistakes
are snare drums and sticks
for you to beat my correction.
I pray my meditation,
my vibration,
my prayers.
my tone
is your wind and brass section
And my life is the stage
you use to orchestrate your song
for my soul's eternal direction.
I pray today is the day
we all seek and find
within our righteous hearts and heavenly
thoughts,
a renewing of our minds,
where we learned that love conquers all
And the love of God unites us all
where we stand
and never again will we divide or fall.
Amen

A Love Affair With The Moon

I can't wait to see you tonight,
all dressed up in satin white
sitting in pitch darkness,
reflecting back at me
your luminous smile
that gives a radiant light
to the night,
staring directly into my eyes.
Just your presence
tells me the truth,
although I am being told
lies to live by
The sight of you
puts me in a trance
It feels my thoughts
with romance.
I would like to get closer to you
if I had the chance,
but I don't and that's alright
because I get to see you
almost each and every night
and before I lay me down to sleep,
I fall to my knees and pray
because I got to say
you're a beautiful sight to see.

Love At First Sight

From the very moment
her eyes met mine
my thoughts said coincidence,
but my heart said it was a sure sign.
She was sitting at a table alone
sipping on some wine
I caught a brother scoping her out,
so I knew I couldn't waste any time
I said to her,
excuse me Miss,
is your table meant for two?
she said to me,
yes it is
I've been sitting here waiting for you!
while looking up at me
with her beautiful brown eyes
it was then I began to feel
something strong and warm deep inside.
Could this be love at first sight
or did we meet for just one night?
Could this be love at first sight
or did we meet for only one night?
We sat and we talked
for an hour or two
and then she asked me

was there something else
I wanted to do
I replied,
let's take a ride
so we drove to the beach
and walked along the seashore
while the water rushed up to our feet,
Walking side-by-side
she took my hand
and looked up to the sky
as if she was thanking God
she found her man.
Could this be love at first sight
or did we meet for just one night?
Could this be love at first sight
or did we meet for only one night?
We laid in the sand
and gazed at the moon.
The sound of the ocean
became our favorite tune
she said it was late
and she would have to leave soon,
but she didn't want the night to end
because she asked me
to come back to her room.
She played some mellow music
and spoke profoundly of her spirituality
I feel my life is finally complete
and she was the only missing piece.

Could this be love at first sight
or did we meet for just one night?
Could this be love at first sight
or did we meet for only one night?

Life Is A Mystery To Me

You didn't plan the hour your life began,
and no one knows
when their final hour will be,
which is why life is a mystery to me.
You know what yesterday was
but you don't know what tomorrow will be
so I live today
in a way
God would be pleased with me
If this is my last day,
can you feel me?
Life is more than just what you can see
It's about feeling the wind blow
and not knowing where it goes
or seeing the raindrops
and not knowing if they're going to stop,
it's about the divine power of the Creator
and how it affects man's behavior.
It's about going deep within your soul
finding your role
and accomplishing your goals
and what purpose your role may unfold
only the future knows
However,
we are blessed with a memory

to remind us how things used to be
now can you see
why life is a mystery to me?
you know what yesterday was
because of your memory
but you don't know
what tomorrow will be
unless it's prophecy
so a prophet you would have to be
I pray God bless us all
and I end this in peace!

Good Lord

Lord, I apologize for the sins I commit
for them I fall to my knees and repent
Lord I thank you for your son Jesus Christ,
who died on the cross so that I may have life,
Lord, I thank you for being with me
every step of the way
watching over your people
day by day
Lord, I thank you for being with me
through my trials and tribulations.
You are my Lord and Savior
because I am your creation
Lord, you are worthy to be praised
from me, that's what you'll get
for the rest of my days
Lord there is nothing I can give you
that can compare to what you've given me,
but I give you my heart, my love, my soul
your Holy Spirit will forever live within me.
Amen.

I Can't Wait

I can't wait
to hold you in my arms again
my strong embrace
would be compatible
to what I feel for you within.
I can't wait to feel
your lips upon mine.
That very moment
would be a gift
bestowed upon me
from father time
I can't wait
until the moment
your eyes meet mine
the thought of your beauty
they would reflect
makes me thank God
I'm not blind
I can't wait
until we spend
the rest of our lives together,
taking love and romance
to a higher level
of degree
just you and me,

our love goes deeper
than the deepest sea,
and higher
than the naked eyes can see.
My love the waiting stops now,
because these thoughts
are kept safely in my heart,
which is where you would always be.

Sunday

It didn't start out
like any ordinary day
She was very unhappy
and I can see it in her face
we were having Sunday's breakfast
when she said there was something
she wanted to say
that this was the beginning of the end,
and we should go our separate ways.
Why do you want to leave me alone
when my love for you is true and strong.
Why do you want to go separate ways
when I dedicate to you
all the hours in my days.
I wanted her to hold me
and not treat me like a friend
and I didn't want to hear her say
that our love was at an end
over and over again
I begged her not to do this to me.
She said she couldn't go on anymore
with me was not where she wanted to be.
Why do you want to leave me alone
when my love for you is true and strong.
How can you just leave me like this

when throwing away true love
for a new friend is a risk.
Then it came to me
in a dream Sunday night
I put you before my Lord
and in my heart that wasn't right
now I can see
why you weren't good for me.
I dedicated my life to you
when it didn't belong to me.
Why do you want to leave me alone
when my love for you is true and strong
now deep in my heart
I truly understand
I should seek the love of God
before the love of any woman.

Today Is The Day

Today is the day
I take this world by surprise
with knowledge and wisdom
representing me
so I can go deep
to the core
where most men
have never gone before
where the heat
doesn't phase me
melanin in my skin galore.
I've adapted to this habitat.
I'm here
then I'm gone like that
I'll creep up on you
like a rat
you'll be frightened
like the elephant
Blood shots of confidence
up in my eyes
you can run
but you cannot hide
wherever you're at
so am I
you want to get away

go ahead and try.
Because I"m coming
and the world is my prey
and I'm hunting
there's no need for running
because I'm coming
and I will not stop
until the world's on the bottom
and I'm standing on top.
Yes, today is the day
I hit this world hard
with the speed of a meteor
and the impact of an asteroid
darkness, void you'll go down
TKO the first round
toe to toe, blow for blow
hurricanes, tornadoes
send your best
I won't fall
Picture this lil man
still standing tall
like that great wall
in China.
If you hide,
I will find ya
so it's best that you stand
and take this whippin like a man.
Because I'm coming
and the world is my prey

and I'm hunting
there's no need for running
because I'm coming
And I will not stop
until the world's on the bottom
and I'm standing on top.
Yes, today is the day
the world is under my control.
No more witches,
no more trolls
no more haters,
no more foes
peaceful men,
loving women.
Let's stop taking
and start giving
let's teach our children
in the homes
What is right
and what is wrong
let's put knowledge and wisdom
in their domes
until they're grown
on their own.
It's up to us,
the time is now
a new world is coming
the old one is going down.
Because I'm coming

And the world is my prey
and I'm hunting
There's no need for running
because I'm coming
and I will not stop
until the world is on the bottom
and I'm standing on top.

A Letter To The devil

Dear dirty devil,
you don't think I can feel or see
how you try to maneuver in my life,
trying to seduce me with your harlots
so that I can commit adultery on my wife
you're a low-down backstabber,
trying to stab me in the back with your knife
or is it a pitchfork you use
when you're creeping in the nights
Whatever tools you try and use
really doesn't matter
because my hopes and dreams
are protected by genes
that I've inherited from my ancestors
who were strong, black, kings, and queens.
Who used spiritual rituals
to fight off you and your dirty schemes.
What did you think
centuries later we would change
because we were taken into bondage
and locked down with chains
don't you know that their blood
is the same blood flowing in my veins
Their thoughts of your defeat,
are the same thoughts

embedded into my brain.
Sure we were brought to a strange land
and given strange names,
but our spiritual essence
will always remain the same.
I admit you have many pieces,
but we are the strongest
piece to this game
and we're gonna continue to
come down on you
like 40 days and 40 nights
of hard, cold rain.
Sincerely,
Andrew Guidry Jr.

www.ingramcontent.com/pod-product-compliance
Lightning Source LLC
LaVergne TN
LVHW050941200726
843508LV00011B/2406